Redeemed: Stripped Down and Unfiltered

Tanya Burns

BookLeaf Publishing

Redeemed: Stripped Down and Unfiltered

Presentation by *BookLeaf Publishing*

Web: www.bookleafpub.com

E-mail: info@bookleafpub.com

ISBN: 9789357696807

First edition 2023

DEDICATION

To my loving husband Joe, who loved a broken mess like me, and thought I was worth the fight. I love you.

ACKNOWLEDGEMENT

This book would have never happened without the Holy Spirit's influence. To Him, the Father, and the Son I give all the glory!

The Prophetic

Pursue [this] love [with eagerness, make it your goal], yet earnestly desire and cultivate the spiritual gifts [to be used by believers for the benefit of the Church], but especially that you may prophesy [to foretell the future, to speak a new message from God to the people]. 1 Corinthians 14:1 AMP

All believers are meant to speak worth His word
However, this ability and gift must be stirred
You first must learn to hear His voice
Among all the chatter and the noise
Allowing yourself to learn
The more you practice, the more you will discern
What it is He wants to say
Through you if you submit and obey

Prophesy is also a spiritual gift
One we should most desire and not dismiss
This gift is meant to edify, exhort, and comfort the Church
Making Jesus known to all who have searched
Far and wide for a touch of heaven
This gift is a valuable weapon

For the words that are spoken are His not mine
I am merely human, but God is divine
I am simply the vessel
An ordinary woman seeking the extraordinary
life, no one special

I operate at a high level in the prophetic
As He speaks to me in rhythm and rhymes, very
poetic
My gift is meant to be shared
God's heart made known; His word declared

Excuse me while I take up space
I have a job to do and that's to run my race
As I introduce to you the One who is filled with
grace
May His words find their way into your heart
Bringing what you need for your fresh start
The extraordinary life awaits you
Don't ever forget Who you belong to

Secret Place (A prophetic word)

"O my dove, [here] in the clefts in the rock,
In sheltered and secret place of the steep pathway,
Let me see your face,
Let me hear your voice;
For your voice is sweet,
And your face is lovely."
Song of Solomon 2:14 AMP

Come away with Me to our secret place
Where we can meet face to face
I have so much to show you, tell you
If only you would step into My grace

As the weight of the world pushes down upon you
And your circumstances cry out for you to make a move
I provide a reprieve for your weary soul
A secret place where you can be made whole

Many of My children are afraid to spend time with Me in this way

For fear that I will reject what they have to say
Knowing My heart for you is key
For this very revelation is what will set you free

How can I get you to see, to understand
That My ways are not the ways of man
For I am for you and not against you
And My love for you will make you anew

I am a God of love
My thoughts are set on the heavenly things above
Come with Me to our secret place
Where I will teach you at your own pace

Don't listen to the lies of your enemy
As he tries to pull you out of communion with Me
For the battle is already won and the victory is yours
So move with Me as we are one accord

Come away with Me to our secret place
As you are learning to receive My grace
What I will give you in return
Will ignite embers that continuously burn

Innocence Stolen

He heals the brokenhearted and binds up their wounds [healing their pain and comforting their sorrow].
Psalms 147:3 AMP

I was between the ages of four and five
When I learned that life wasn't meant for living, but a thing you just survive
By the actions of one sick man
Satan began his strategic plan
My life would change forever that day
As I was left shattered and in a state of dismay

Laying in bed tucked in all snug and tight
Staring at the wall despite it being late at night
I could hear the party raging just outside my door
Just as I had time and time before

I was finally drifting off to sleep
Due to counting sheep after sheep
When my door flung wide open
The atmosphere suddenly became less than Zen

The smell of alcohol and weed was so strong

Every fiber in my little body was screaming somethings wrong
Gripping tightly to my stuffed bunny, I began to pray
That whoever it was would just go away

Unfortunately, that wasn't the case
As I felt his arms wrap me in a strong embrace
His hands and mouth were all over me
I kept my eyes tightly closed not wanting to see
The pain was unbearable as his rhythm became more intense
Despite all the noise no one came to my defense

I don't know how much time went by
All I know was that I just wanted to die
Spirit crushed, mind fractured, my body violated
Satan wanted me out of the picture, annihilated

Once his assault of me was complete,
He left my room rejoining the party, never missing a beat
Hearing the door shut, the tears began to flow
I made a vow to myself after what my body had to undergo
That I never again would myself to feel
And my sweet tender heart became one of steel

He would not be the last man to come to me
with their vicious assault
And I came into agreement with the lie that it
was all my fault
My mind learned how to disconnect
To self-protect

By the age of six I was completely numb
And would stay that way for years to come
Yet I had a covering I didn't even know about
As Jesus was working on my way out

I would be in my thirties before I saw His plan
manifest
And my spirit yield finally able to rest
Despite the pain and all I had been through
His love and purpose for me where beginning to
come into view
He chose me before I chose Him
And I began to see the light even though it was
still dim

If your story sounds a lot like mine
Take heart in knowing that you still can shine
And better days are coming up ahead
Because my dear you are not the tail but the
head
Jesus has a plan while you are here on this earth

Allow Him to love you through the pain and show you your worth
I promise you, you won't regret it
As God begins to heal you bit by bit
His love is relentless and pure
A safe place to hide, to feel secure
Don't give up before the miracle takes place
Allow yourself to be immersed in His grace
This is my prayer for you
That one day you will find healing too

Lost to Found

Jesus said to him, “I am the [only] way [to God] and the [real] Truth and the [real] Life; no one comes to the Father but through Me." John 14:6 AMP

When I was a child, I lived in a world of fantasy
Because I didn’t know how to cope with what had been done to me
This world I had created for myself wasn’t so bad
At least here I had a present and sober mom and dad
It wasn’t until I started school that I began to realize, that my life didn’t look like that of my peers
So, I withdrew more into my own little world which would last into my adult years

This world of mine was safe, one where I had complete control
It was a place of comfort and brought peace to my young, tormented soul
As my fantasies became more exquisite, the deeper I would retreat

Unbeknownst to me, my two worlds where
about to meet

Wanting to just be normal and accepted
The words came out in a way I hadn't expected
Looking back I'm not really surprised
The pain was mounting and could no longer be
disguised.
"My mother is dead", I blurted out to my first
grade class--
The room fell silent, and I just wanted the
moment to pass
Even in my innocence and youth
I was able to discern that this lie had to be better
than the truth
Which was my mother was in prison due to her
addiction
And my father was a drunk off somewhere
unknown dealing with his own afflictions

My grandparents were called, the damage
already done
The school recommended that I speak with
someone
It was there during my therapy sessions
That my soul fell into a deep oppression
I began to create someone who had a voice, a
choice even though she wasn't real

To the outside world she was the one who was
more ideal

Satan comes to kill, steal, and destroy
And he used my invented persona as part of his
ploy
She got to walk around happy and free
While I was living a life trapped in hell and
bound in misery
All of this occurred before the tender age of ten
As I was already enslaved to the approval of
men

I continued this way as the years went by
Not knowing that God had a plan, I was
introduced to a guy
It was days before I turned seventeen
Little did I know Jesus was about to come on the
scene
This boy that I had just met could never have
known
The impact it would have on my life when he
began to speak of the Chief Corner Stone

The way he spoke of Jesus made Him feel so
real
And the conviction stirring in my heart made me
see that the way I was living was less than ideal
The Father can't be found, He must be revealed

And as He did so with me, my spirit began to
yield
I wanted all this man Jesus had to give
As I asked Him into my heart, He was quick to
forgive

The way I felt in that moment I will never forget
A decision was made, one I will never regret
This is where my journey with Jesus began
As He called to me and said, "My daughter let
Me show you My plan
This is just the beginning of your story.
I will use you greatly for My glory."

I wish I could tell you after this things were all
peachy keen
But sadly, many things would take place that I
could have never foreseen
I invite you to come along with me
On a journey, one marked with great love and
intimacy
As I let the walls down that surround my heart
Of how God took a sinner like me and set her
apart

Training Ground

And not only this, but [with joy] let us exult in our sufferings and rejoice in our hardships, knowing that hardship (distress, pressure, trouble) produces patient endurance; and endurance, proven character (spiritual maturity); and proven character, hope and confident assurance [of eternal salvation]. Romans 5:3-4 AMP

The man who introduced me to Jesus
Would become my first husband
If only you could have seen us
Young, free, in love and
Totally blind to what lied ahead
A future of joys, sorrows, and dread

He made me a mother to three wonderful boys
This was one of my few joys
Out of ten years of marriage
Which ended in despair and wreckage

As hard as it was, it was not wasted time
It was meant to be part of God's design
Writing this with no intent of placing blame
This is merely a purging and my way to reclaim

Everything the enemy has stolen
Proclaiming His truth till every curse is broken
Off my life and the ones I love
Ascending on my bloodline like a dove

He was my first with many things
Lots of rebellion and a long list of sins
My life before him was very sheltered
And as the tension rose in my home I weltered

With the creation of life
Came a huge blow out and massive fight
This was the out I had been waiting for
Unplanned and not expected, I just couldn't take
it anymore

I traded one environment for another
Not realizing what I soon would uncover
A man who was just as damaged as I was
Who lived by his own selfish needs and the
motto just because

Our life together took us to Arizona
Where he yet again would take on another
persona
His trauma would soon begin to trigger mine
And so began our descent into a steady decline

Before we hit rock bottom came baby number two
I thought for sure he would be the glue
That could put us back together
And our family of four would be better than ever

How I was sadly mistaken
I couldn't believe the things I would partaken
As my misery grew
I began to resent him; all he would say and do

His control of me grew worse
And my responses to others coerced
I had no one left who cared
He made sure of that, I was trapped, ensnared

He lied, manipulated, and cheated
I had come to accept this is how a wife should be treated
I wasn't much better back then
My rage coming out again and again

What were we thinking as we came to decide
That baby number three could bridge the great divide
Bringing us back to each other
Looking back our stupidity makes me shudder

Still, we tried to make it work for many more years
With three little ones in toe, I was still trying to calm his fears
But all my attempts would fall short
Once again in the arms of another woman he would resort

We decided to call it quits
I was being tested, more than I could admit
I thought I was going to live the life I wanted
But instead, my soul became more bound and haunted
As I began a dance with the devil
That led to my demise at so many levels

Seeing his happiness with her more in-depth
I retreated deeper into the bowels of death
I just wanted to go numb
Feeling the betrayal from the two of them
Finding out she would have his son
I gave into the pain coming completely undone

*This undoing of me has its own story
Once again God gets all the glory
Nothing from this marriage was wasted
As this is where the foundation was created
A series of events, the perfect storm

Turning me into someone I no longer knew,
completely transformed*

Looking back at that time now
I understand why God had to allow
The two of us to do what we did
All the mistakes we made with our kids
Every trial meant to bend me towards Him
Knowing the light in my eyes would go dim

Yet still there was a flicker
And after years a clear picture
Of what my ex-husband had gave me
A very personal experience of how not to be
If I wanted any of my relationships to work
I'm sorry if that hurts, I'm really trying to not
come off like a jerk
I learned from both our actions
Each of us chasing our own dragons

My ex-husband gave me a wonderful gift
He was part of my training ground where I
became equipped
To walk into the woman I'm becoming
With each passing day I can hear the drumming
Of the warrior deep inside
As one day she would let out a wail, a cry
My Battle Cry was being formed
And in the fire, I was forged

Into whom I am now
I bid you ado, taking my bow

Battle Cry

Put on the full armor of God [for His precepts are like the splendid armor of a heavily armed solider], so that you may be able to [successfully] stand up against all schemes and strategies and the deceits of the devil.
Ephesians 6:11 AMP

Bruised, battered, and bloody is my current state
As my heart cries Lord I can't take this weight
Yet You continue to allow the onslaught to take place
Quietly reminding me that I live under Your grace

Divine purpose seems so far from my reach
But You say my victory is found within my speech
How can this be when the words just aren't there
And all I see is a pit of despair

Death swirls around me in this season
You keep telling me that You have Your reasons
It's not just self that I am having to lie down
It is everything that sets itself higher than You and Your crown

Why must I endure this vicious fight
When all I want is to be in Your glorious light
You whisper, "This too shall pass
But not until I reach the masses."

From the depths of my very being comes a cry
One I can no longer hold back even if I try
Deep down it begins to rise to the back of my
throat
Bringing about a sound to which there is no note
A series of grunts and groans bubble up out of
me
You say this is the process in which I must walk
to become free
I begin to feel death's grip slowly releasing
And Your Spirit which resides in me increasing

As I surrender deeper than I have ever known
My life begins to take on a different tone
Hell made a mistake coming after me
My faith is planted like a firm oak tree

For this is my Battle Cry I give to the Lord
Taking up my shield and the Word which is my
sword
So devil you better run
Because the Lord and I have just begun!

From Addict to Mouthpiece: Part 1 of 2

For I do not understand my own actions [I am baffled and bewildered by them]. I do not practice what I want to do, but I am doing the very thing I hate [and yielding to my human nature, my worldliness – my sinful capacity]. Romans 7:15 AMP

Dope fiend, addict, worthless whore
These were the names I gave my reflection
Every time I would use my body in ways it wasn't created for
Praying I would just fade away with the next injection

Wasted, high, and completely strung out
Was how I was living my life
When all I wanted to do was shout,
"God please just release me from this internal strife."

Yet my prayers would go unheard
Every time I was revived
Back at it again, eyes drooped, vision blurred

Crying out to Jesus, "Why do you keep letting me survive!?"

I didn't wait around for an answer
Instead I would go back to chasing that high
Even though it was more deadly than cancer
I wouldn't be satisfied until I had an endless supply

So, I keep putting a needle in my vein
Over and over because of what it would bring
A way to escape my trauma and pain
To me at the time this was a good, good thing

I lied to myself saying I just didn't care
That this monster had taken everything from me
The truth was too much to bear
In fact, it had stolen my ability to be a mother of three

I hated myself more with each passing day
I was broken, no shattered to be more precise
And had come to accept this was the price I had to pay
For all the evil I had done and having a heart that was cold as ice

I was engaged to a man I didn't want to marry
But I continued to act and put on a show

One night in the tub thought after thought I would bury
Until one popped up, “You will marry a man named Joe.”

(See that thought wasn’t mine I so clearly heard
It was the voice of the Holy Spirit who dwells inside
He gives us the power to obey and walk out the Word
This voice I could not bury no matter how hard I tried.)

This was not the man who’s ring I wore on my finger
Drying off I raced to the kitchen for another hit
Yet this name continued to linger
As I drifted off into that pitch dark pit

Day after day I continued to use
Unaware of how God was moving in my favor
Until one day I no longer could take his abuse
So I left not knowing how my heart would waiver

My “friend” Joe took me in, it still hadn’t clicked
Hope began setting into my soul
Even though this habit had yet to be kicked

And I was losing more and more self control

My ex that I had just recently left
Hung around like a stink in the air
I allowed it to happen so I must carry this heft
As I continued on with my affair

My life carried on this way for nine months time
Joe and I had married and were preparing to move
Having paid a steep price for our crime
Things were just about to improve

I had hit my rock bottom and was ready to surrender
To the pleas and cries of family and my soul-mate
My heart now open to the love of the one who I would know as my Defender
God's pursuit of me was not up for debate

I was introduced to a place called Celebrate Recovery
As soon as I walked in I knew I had found my tribe
They loved Jesus and truly wanted to help me
So I dove all in honestly digging the vibe

CR was held at the Village Community Church

It was here on a Friday night of prayer
That at last I no longer had to search
For my purpose here, God said my job would be quiet rare

With a single word Jesus changed the trajectory of my course
This addict was about to be turned into God's mouthpiece
A Proverbs 31 woman whom God would be proud to endorse
His words one day, I would release
And my life would go from lack to abundant increase

Letting Go

"Whenever you stand praying, if you have something against anyone, forgive him [drop the issue, let it go], so that your Father who is in heaven will also forgive you your transgressions and wrongdoings [against Him and others]. [But if you do not forgive, neither will your Father in heaven forgive your transgressions."] Mark 11:25-26 AMP

You came into my life at my lowest point
My weaknesses you would gladly exploit
Build me up just to tear me back down
You called me your queen and in the same breath tore at my crown
You lied and would manipulate
It didn't take long for me to reciprocate
All the red flags were there
Yet I ignored them completely aware
Of who you were on the inside
Someone filled with spite and pride
A darkness in your soul
I thought I could change you and make you whole
This was my first mistake
Your influence for years I could not shake

You had my mind so confused and warped
Everything I said you would distort
Keeping me up for days at a time
Wasn't even close to your worst crime
Gaslighting and making me think I was crazy
Was just some of the abuse you dealt out daily

Then came the time you would manifest
You were not you, but a man possessed
For the evil in you that day did prevail
As the words came out, they would for sure derail
My walk with the Lord and my destiny
Coming into agreement with the lie you spoke over me

Even after you were gone your words would linger
Saying your name had become a trigger
How do I take back my power
And be able to say "the name" without looking like I ate something sour

I knew what I needed to do, and it didn't make me happy
In fact, it made me feel mad and crappy
I needed to forgive you
The truth was becoming more apparent and harder for me to chew

You caused so much damage and destruction
Yet Jesus was very clear with His instruction

He will forgive me if I forgive others
If not, then I am the one who suffers
I no longer want to carry this weight
Of unforgiveness, revenge, and hate
Wherever you are I want you to know
I forgive you and no longer see you as my foe
May God bless you; Jesus loves you more than
you will ever know

From Addict to Mouthpiece:
Part 2 of 2

We love, because He first loved us. 1 John 4:19 AMP

Overcoming my addiction was just the beginning
I had a lot of skeletons and junk in my trunk
I quickly realized I had to be willing
If I wanted to become unstuck

I began to work the twelve steps
While also going through Discipleship School
Amazed at how the two would intersect
Each one a precious gift but also a tool

God was setting the foundation of our relationship
Knowing the drugs were just some fruit
The more He made me equipped
The closer to the surface He brought the root

Co-dependency, people pleasing, and control
Trauma, anxiety, and fear of rejection
All these manifesting in my soul
Like a deadly infection

This is where my bondage truly lied
It would take years of healing
Before I began to humble my heart, letting go of my pride
Allowing Jesus to be the one doing the revealing

Who I am, what I was created for
He spoke early on in my journey
But for years I chose to ignore
Because I didn't see myself as worthy

So, I began to run from my calling
Hoping God would change His mind
I was just stalling
He became more inclined
To show His love for me
This I could not fight
As His love took root sprouting like a tree
It took hold of my heart with much delight

His love kept bringing me back
Even when I didn't want this voice
In Him there is nothing I lack
Yet I was the one who had to make the choice

Accepting my call meant I must obey
And give all control over
Doing so without delay

Laying it all bare, my complete exposure

He knew it all anyhow
That wasn't the point
The more chaos God would allow
The more areas of my life He began to anoint

His gifts He gave abundantly
Even as I still struggled
To live my life triumphantly
He chuckled while I stayed puzzled

I had to unlearn everything I thought I knew
Religion was never His plan
How easy it is for people to misconstrue
His Word, this is the ways of man

Relationship was what He was after
All of me, bad habits included
Intimacy with Him is what would shatter
All the habits that kept me secluded

God chose me not despite my past
But because of it
For it created in me a resilience, one that would last
And a spirit that would yield to Him and willfully submit

Metamorphosis

"No one puts new wine into old wineskins; otherwise the [fermenting] wine will [expand and] burst the skins, and the wine is lost as well as the wineskins. But new wine must be put into new wineskins." Mark 2:22 AMP

Stripped down bare, naked, and vulnerable
Rawness oozing out of every pore
Weighing the cost of the inevitable
A shaking to her very core

How can she let go of the old version of herself
Or is that the point of this cocoon
As You tenderly take her off of this shelf
To make her bold and immune

She speaks with such wisdom and grace
A consuming fire burning in her chest
The world wants her to know her place
But You raise her up amidst the protest

She fights desperately to hold on to what she knows
Weariness soaking into her bones

Yet You continue to empower her younger self
to grow
Releasing a power as her spirit moans

Her heart is shifting into a place of authority
Her mind becomes a fortress of peace
She will no longer take part in the conformity
And she begins to operate out of a place of
increase

Hell quivers with fear as she finds her place in
the Kingdom
Demons flee as she steps into her identity
No longer will she listen to the lies that she is a
victim
And her life becomes filled with a deep serenity

As she looks back at the tremendous fight over
her soul
She sees how important it was that she doesn't
give up
So without hesitation she gives up complete
control
And allows You to overflow her cup

The result becomes life changing not just for her
By the multitudes a deeper understanding of You
shall be revealed

They will no longer be able to stay as they once
were
As You bring her forth finally unconcealed

The price was great but her desire for You
trumps all
Looking back she would do it all again
Without question she knows she won't fall
And with that she shouts an Amen!

Waiting (A prophetic word)

But those who wait for the Lord [who expect, look for, and hope in Him] will gain new strength and renew their power; they will lift up their wings [and rise up close to God] like eagles [rising toward the sun]; they will run and not become weary, they will walk and not grow tired. Isaiah 40:31 AMP

I have spoken many promises to you
And as time goes by you fight to believe if I will come through
I see you growing weary and tired
Yet your faith is one to be admired
As you have never let go
Of My promises deep within your soul
    Your season of waiting is coming to an end
No more hope deferred as My outpouring of blessings begins
I had to get you to a place to receive
All that was coming, more than you could ever believe
    Timing is truly the key
Because too much too soon would cause you to depart from Me

I have known you before you were in your
mother's womb
That's why My blessings never come too late or
too soon
In the waiting, in the wilderness
Your heart developed a tenderness
Your mind became quite and clear
You became more aware of My presence and
that I am always near
The scales fell from your eyes
And you finally let go of your disguise
Your skin thickened up, yet your heart has
stayed soft and pure
Resisting Satan's pleas and lures
To stay hidden away in your cave
You chose to rise and be brave
All because your waiting season
Brought about these changes, see I had my
reasons
I had to get you to a place where you would be
ready
And to a point that I was the one keeping you
steady
When the chaos and pain of life hit
That you wouldn't give up and quit
I knew what was inside of you, I placed it
there
I even know the count of each of your hairs

I allowed the pressures of life to bend you toward Me
So I could begin My work of healing, deliverance, and setting you free
I share all of this with you
Because during your walk with Me waiting is something you will always do
It's not how long you wait but how that matters
So rise above all the chatter
And go into waiting with expectation in your heart
Knowing this is where I form My best works of art

Redeemed

Let the redeemed of the Lord say so, Whom He has redeemed from the hand of the adversary Psalms 107:2 AMP

I am redeemed, bought with a price
Jesus bore all my sin, the perfect lamb sacrificed
It should have been me nailed to that cross
But God had a plan, one that would be His greatest loss
Turning away from His son during his greatest pain
Gave me the rights and authority in the Kingdom's domain

I am redeemed because of the blood
That flowed from His body mixing with the mud
Every gash, every wound wide open
His spirit obedient, His body broken
Made it possible for me
To be made right with God, filled with praise and jubilee

I am redeemed, the righteousness of God
Because the Good Shepherd with His staff and rod

Thought I was worth dying for
So He went down to hell and settled the score
Taking back every key
Jesus, His name is power and authority
His name causing demons to shake and flee
This is the same power that now resides in me

I am redeemed, God's beloved
When He looks at me, He sees the blood
My sin cast as far as the east is from the west
In a gown of white is how He sees me dressed
I have been made clean because of the Son
There was nothing I could have said or done
To get this kind of freedom from the evil one

I am redeemed, made brand new
After You I will fervently pursue
For all my days
You will forever have all my praise
Here's my life Lord, put it on display
My spirit shouts, "Jesus have your way!"

Thankful For

Her mother-in-law said to her, "Where did you glean today? Where did you work? Blessed be the man who took notice of you." So she told her mother-in-law with whom she had worked and said, "The name of the man with whom I worked today is Boaz." Ruth 2:19 AMP

I have no words to express
How grateful I am but nevertheless
I will use what words I know
To express my gratitude as your Spirit fills me head to toe
Today is a day of Thanksgiving
I look around at my husband's family all so forgiving
It was many years ago on this day
That my heart issues would be put on display
As my insecurities bubbled to the surface
And I blew up like a furnace
Not my best moment to say the least
I left quickly just wanting to retreat
They will never accept me now
Probably thinking to themselves, "Just wow!"
You knew exactly what you were doing when
You brought Joe into my life

You are the one who impressed on him to ask me to be his wife
It wasn't just him but also his family
Their love, warmth, and hospitality
That helped soften my heart to hear Your voice
And bring about a life I could enjoy
Every time after that
They continued to love me right where I was at
You used them with or without them knowing
To pour love into me until I was overflowing
In my in-laws I had finally found
My family that would help keep me on solid ground
As I sit in admiration of this wonderful gift
I know You are here in our midst
My heart couldn't be more thankful
And my spirit more tranquil
I couldn't ask for more in this moment
Thank you, Jesus, for my in-laws, they were the missing component
My heart needed to flow as Your poet

Step Out

However, you are not [living] in the flesh [controlled by the sinful nature] but in the Spirit, if in fact the Spirit of God lives in you [directing and guiding you]. But if anyone does not have the Spirit of Christ, he does not belong to Him [and is not a child of God]. If Christ lives in you, though your [natural] body is dead because of sin, your spirit is alive because of righteousness [which He provides]. Romans 8:9-10 AMP

This life comes with all kinds of pressures
Too many demands to count
So many go to extreme measures
Making their fears and anxieties mount

The pull, the need to fit into culture
Can and will push people over the edge
One mess up the world encloses like a vulture
No wonder thousands end up on a ledge

What if I told you there was another way to navigate this life
Casting all your fears and anxiety
Onto the One who took on all our sin and strife
Even as we sit in our pride and piety

When you accept Jesus into your heart
The Holy Spirit becomes an indwelling presence
He is the one whom never departs
For He is also omnipresent

Through Him you can operate out of a different realm
Which has always been there, now you have eyes to see
Before you start to get overwhelmed
The Word and His Spirit are the key

The natural and supernatural co-exist
Each having their own set of rules
One has bondage and death on its list
While the other has living water and healing pools

As good as the latter sounds, many Christians choose the former
Because here they don't have to die to self
By escaping the grasp of the Reformer
The Holy Spirit, they just store on a shelf

By doing so they forfeit their power and authority
Living below their means as co-heirs
Sadly, this seems to be the majority

Wondering why they have so many unanswered prayers

It takes boldness and courage to live life in the Spirit
To walk differently than others
Because those you hold dear
Will not understand your true colors

Jesus sees you, accepting you always
Giving you the Holy Spirit to direct your every step
Teaching you His lessons and ways
His promises are true and His words are always kept

Matters of One's Heart (A prophetic word)

But the Lord said to Samuel, "Do not look at his appearance or at the height of his stature, because I have rejected him. For the Lord sees not as man sees; for man looks at the outward appearance, but the Lord looks at the heart." 1 Samuel 16:7 AMP

I love all My children none more or less
Love isn't the factor that sets some apart from the rest
Each one has a function, a purpose in the body
Yet many complain they are sick of being stuck in the lobby
How can I call them out to see from My view
If they aren't even willing to complete what I have already given them to do
Time and time again I have tried to get their attention
And when I bless them I don't even get a mention
It grieves My spirit so
But I am not looking for those who put on a show
I see the heart of every man, woman, and child

I know who is pure and who is defiled
I am the one who decides who gets what gifts
Yet this continues to be the source of so many rifts
So many fail to see and refuse to understand
That if I gave them what they wanted they would be crushed into sand
The gifts aren't what they are truly after, it's the drawing to the anointing
Which comes with a cost, a weight the two closing adjoining
Titles and positions will only go so far
If ones heart and character are not up to par
I require a deep level of intimacy
This is only acquired by spending quality time with Me
Out of this place is where some rise higher than the others
Because they chose to lay down their lives for their sisters and brothers
By emptying their vessels completely, their flesh decreasing
And making plenty of room for My spirit to begin increasing
This pleases Me so and I take much delight
For they used their free will and surrendered the fight
To live a life of consecration
Regardless of the implications

So, the next time someone says they want what you carry
Gently remind them that the gifts and anointing from person to person will vary
But My love for them remains unchanging
And that they were worth saving
I trust you with this because I know you will always point them back to Me
Because in your heart and with your mouth you have given Me all the glory
This is how they will begin to soar
When they allow me to shake them to their very core
Stand firm on their behalf
For I will be the one who has the last laugh
As they begin to fall deeply, madly in love with Me
The anointing will rise like the waves in the sea
A little, a lot that's for Me to decide
One thing is for certain they will always be My Bride

River

Now on the last and most important day of the feast, Jesus stood and called out [in a loud voice], "If anyone is thirsty, let him come to Me and drink! He who believes in Me [who adheres to, trusts in, and relies on Me], as the Scripture has said, 'From his innermost being will flow continually rivers of living water.'" John 7:37-38 AMP

Endless currents of living water
Here is where I hear you say, "Take heart My daughter."
Saturated from head to toe
I should have stepped into these waters long ago

More healing comes to my soul
As I surrender more deeply and give up all control
Still deep waters You said You would create
In me as I learned to carry Your weight
Of who You called me to be
Despite how much I fought You and would disagree

A river that smells like a fresh spring rain

One I never have to leave and can always remain
The abundant life is what Your Spirit offers me
These waters bring a source of power and authority

I must make the choice
To stay how I am or follow Your voice
As You call out to me and say,
"My beloved come this way."
"In this river you and I are one accord
I am the lover of your soul, The Lord
I will instruct you in My ways
Keeping your eyes fixed on My gaze
I want to be able to express Myself more freely
When and how I choose ideally
I have a personality and character traits
I am more than just a voice that guides and navigates
I have thoughts, feelings, and emotions
Have you learned nothing from My Word, teachings, and devotions?
Stop caring what other people think
The River is waiting, come and drink!"

Let us step into the river and soar
Come on Saints what are you waiting for!

The Dance

Make every effort to keep the oneness of the Spirit in the bond of peace [each individual working together to make the whole successful]. Ephesians 4:3 AMP

To and frow
Eb and flow
This shall be our dance
Such intimacy beautiful romance
You move, I move
We have our own little groove
You lead I will follow
I'm never alone never solo
You set the pace
As I gaze into Your face
Never too fast or too slow
Leading me into a life of overflow
As we dance, I fall more in love
We fit together like a hand and a glove
As my spirit becomes more in sync with Yours
This dance of ours grows, becoming more mature
The second guesses are fleeing
As my eyes become more foreseeing
The doubts begin to dissipate

I'm becoming more adapt to anticipate
Where we are headed too next
As everyone watches in amazement but also
perplexed
Our rhythm matching perfectly
So in sync our steps running concurrently
You lead with such grace and elegance
Never with pride or arrogance
You are truly the perfect partner
And I would gladly be a martyr
If it means that our dance never ends
As You are truly the lover of my soul and best
friend

Many Faces of Grief

In this you rejoice greatly, even though now for a little while, if necessary, you have been distressed by various trials, so that the genuineness of your faith, which is perishable, even though tested and purified by fire, may be found to result in [your] praise and glory and honor at the revelation of Jesus Christ. 1 Peter 1:6-7 AMP

Someone I look up to and greatly admire
Spoke about her grief journey leaving me truly inspired
I would like to do the same
Even if it's just one person who decides to walk out of their shame
This is my story and journey with grief
And how by accepting it I was able to turn over a new leaf

Grief comes with the loss of people, places, and things
None are immune to its untimely stings
Most of my losses didn't come with literal death
But each one took me to my knees and took my breath

My innocence stolen, my lost childhood
I saw and experienced more than any child should
The years I spent thinking it was all my fault
Caused me to keep my heart locked in a vault
So much time wasted
Self-loathing and self-hated
I had to grieve that lost wasted time too
It was way long overdue

The abortion I had
That kind of grief will drive you literally mad
This grief alone came with such a weight
Because I took a life God wanted to create
I buried it for as long as I could
But God said, "I will use this for your good."
So I allowed my heart to feel
As Jesus walked me through how to heal

The loss of my first marriage
I was not prepared for the emotional wreckage
As the grief took all control
I never thought again I would be whole
I had failed as a wife
He already moved on to a new life
Here the enemy did some of his best work
As my grief made me look crazy and berserk

Once again, I came out of agreement with the lies
I began to heal as Jesus listened to my cries

A positive pregnancy test
Brought more than worries and stress
Grief of lost hopes and dreams
There went my chance at playing on a college basketball team
I knew the chance I was taking
With each act of love making
Yet grief still settled in my soul
As I felt my life was ruined and out of control
I had to accept this new future I had
Though I was mourning, dare I say mad

I missed so much time with my children whey they were little
Drugs stole that time of sweet kisses and giggles
This grief left me completely undone, wrecked
For I had seven years to sit and reflect
Of the damage done, all the lost time
Would they ever forgive me for my crimes
In time, I learned to forgive myself
Forgiveness is full of riches and wealth
But I had to come to terms that I was grieving
Before I could pour out, I must be receiving
God's love, mercy, and grace

So I could give to my children when we would meet face to face

When God called me to the five-fold
I felt a loss of total control
For me I knew what this meant
And what my life would now represent
Die to self, a price to pay
I was to surrender all and obey
I just wanted to be normal, to fit in
Grief began to rise deep from within
Of what I thought my life should be
And it didn't matter how loud I would plea
God wouldn't take this cup from me

Grief isn't something to just get over
Done right, it brings God closer
He is near to the brokenhearted
Through your grief He has already charted
Your way to move through and forward
Standing firm on His promises and Word
So, take Him at it, His word I mean
And He will teach you how to navigate through grief's ravine

Deliverance

And He was saying to them all, "If anyone wishes to follow Me [as My disciple], he must deny himself [set aside selfish interests], and take up his cross daily [expressing a willingness to endure whatever may come] and follow Me [believing in Me, conforming to My example in living and, if need be, suffering or perhaps dying because of faith in Me]." Luke 9:23 AMP

To speak worth Your words requires humility
A pure heart and clean hands
And a great amount of sensibility
To Your voice to give Your commands

Here is where I found my threshing
As You began a good work in me
Through the process of the pressing
A new wine for all to taste and see

Every trial was a part of my training ground
Every battle had its purpose
My mind and spirit becoming unified and sound
Even with the pain You were drawing to the surface

Jesus, you were getting to the very core
Of my pain, and You would bring a deliverance
That would cause my wings to spread so I could
soar
No longer did I want to stay in a state of
belligerence

I gave in to You as I received Your love
Gave You all control saying, "Lord use me how
You see fit
I want to speak Your truth in love
All my life and ways to You I commit."

You showed up in a mighty way
One I was not expecting
Your power and glory on full display
As I began to vomit, physically rejecting
The spirit of rejection which had plagued me
Manifesting fruit not of God, I used my prayer
language and began to decree
Your word to that thing, my flesh submitting no
longer in dispute
Giving myself fully to Your pursuit

From that moment on
The words flowed from my pen
I have given up the con
No longer catering to the acceptance of men

With the writing of these words
I will never again have to look back
Each poem written my heart confirms
Your truth of this, never again will I lack

Once this book is complete
The old me, the past will be done
Never again shall the two meet
As I, God's mouthpiece has just begun
To introduce you to Jesus, God's one and only
Son

In Me (A prophetic word)

Therefore as you have received Christ Jesus the Lord, walk in [union with] Him [reflecting His character in the things you do and say – living lives that lead others away from sin], having been deeply rooted [in Him] and now being continually built up in Him and [becoming increasingly more] established in your faith, just as you were taught, and overflowing in it with gratitude. Colossians 2:6-7 AMP

In Me you will find peace
A safe place where you can release
All your worry and cares to Me
As you walk out your victory

In Me you will find rest
As you pass your test
Of trusting Me with it all
As you respond to My call

In Me you will find comfort
My tender embrace the enemy can't pervert
I will heal your shattered heart
From the brokenhearted I shall never depart

In Me you will find a friend
A helping hand I will lend
Closer than a brother I will be
To those who choose to follow willingly

In Me you will find freedom
You life will take on new meaning
Trusting the grueling process
I make a message from your mess

In Me you will find acceptance
As you learn to confess and walk in repentance
Knowing you are under My grace
As you live and run your race

In Me you will find love
Because I am love
Loving you right where you are at
My love never fails this is a fact

In Me you will find all you need
I hear you cry, beg, and plead
I'm about to release My favor
Never again will your faith waiver

www.ingramcontent.com/pod-product-compliance
Lightning Source LLC
Chambersburg PA
CBHW062147160726
48282CB00027B/954

9789357696807